中華雋詞

初大告選譯

CHINESE LYRICS

Translated by CH'U TA-KAO

With a preface by

SIR ARTHUR QUILLER-COUCH

1937 · CAMBRIDGE: At the
UNIVERSITY PRESS

CAMBRIDGE
UNIVERSITY PRESS

32 Avenue of the Americas, New York NY 10013-2473, USA

Cambridge University Press is part of the University of Cambridge.

It furthers the University's mission by disseminating knowledge in the pursuit of
education, learning and research at the highest international levels of excellence.

www.cambridge.org
Information on this title: www.cambridge.org/9781107418615

© Cambridge University Press 1937

This publication is in copyright. Subject to statutory exception
and to the provisions of relevant collective licensing agreements,
no reproduction of any part may take place without the written
permission of Cambridge University Press.

First published 1937
First paperback edition 2014

A catalogue record for this publication is available from the British Library

ISBN 978-1-107-41861-5 Paperback

Cambridge University Press has no responsibility for the persistence or accuracy of
URLs for external or third-party internet websites referred to in this publication,
and does not guarantee that any content on such websites is, or will remain, accurate
or appropriate.

To

VICTOR G. KIERNAN

CONTENTS

Preface   *page* xi

WEI CHUANG (A.D. 850?–910)
  The South Country   1

NIU HSI-CHI (*c.* 925)
  For Remembrance   2

FÊNG YEN-CHI (*d.* 960)
  Her Birthday   3

PRINCE LI YÜ (936–978)
  The Fisherman's Song   4
  Court Life   5
  The Tryst   6
  Past and Present   7
  Separation   8
  A Love-Song   9
  Regrets   10
  Longing for the South Country   11
  The Land of Drunkenness   12
  The Everlasting Sorrow   13

FAN CHUNG-YEN (989–1052)
  On the Frontier   14

SUNG CH'I (998–1061)
  To a Friend   15

LIU YUNG (*c.* 990–1050)
  Parting in Autumn   16
  Home Thoughts   17

ANONYMOUS
 A Blossom   18

OU-YANG HSIU (1007–1072)
 In the First Full-moon Night   19

WANG AN-SHIH (1021–1086)
 A Farewell   20

SU SHIH (1036–1101)
 After Drinking   21
 In Memory   22
 Drinking in the Mid-autumn Night 23
 On the Red Cliff   24
 A Plan for the Future   25
 Where Travellers Go   26
 The Recluse   27
 The Home-coming   28

YEH CH'ING-CH'ÊN (c. 1030)
 Peony Time   30

CH'IN KUAN (1049–1100)
 The Seventh Night of the Seventh Moon 31

LI CH'ING-CHAO (1081–1140?)
 Weighed Down   32

CHU TUN-JU (1080–1175)
 Plum-Blossoms   33
 Sorrow and Flowers   34
 Leaning on the Balustrades 35
 The Golden Days   36
 Leisure   37
 Old Age   38

Li Chih-yi (*c.* 1100)
A River-long Love   39

Hsiang Kao (*c.* 1100)
Solitude   40

Lü-ch'iu Tz'ŭ-kao
On the River   41

Hsin Ch'i-chi (1140–1207)
In my Carousal   42
Now I know   43
To the Moon at the Mid-autumn Night   44
Walking by the Stream   45
My Sorrow   46
Life in the Cup   47
To my Children   48

Liu K'ê-chuang (1187–1269)
Absence   49
Flowery Questions   50

Kuan Chien
Spring   51

Kuan Tao-shêng (*c.* 1250)
You and I   52

Liu Yin (1249–1293)
Drinking beneath the Blossoming Trees   53

Bhikshu Chêng Yen (*c.* 1700)
The Master of the Western Lakes   54

PREFACE

IT is with extreme diffidence that I introduce this small
volume of translations by my friend Mr Ch'u Ta-kao;
myself knowing nothing of the Chinese language and only
so much about its poetry as I have gathered from ren-
derings by other hands, and by listening eagerly to those
who explained—whether in books or talk—its develop-
ment in technique and its more constant ethical principles.

Of its technique—even apart from its straight-laced
forms, its parallel appeal to ear and eye (so that to the
Chinese, with their ideographics, the very calligraphy
counts in their esteem of a lyric, or of a distich with a
flower as companion ornament of a silken scroll or a vase)—
I can only say the obvious thing and hazard a guess upon it.
Quite obviously our tradition of stress and rhyme will
never suit the Chinese lyric, whether to translate or to
copy with any conveyance of its peculiar beauty: for the two
work on different planes, ours accentual, the Chinese *tonal*.
Yet our language in the daily speech of all classes is
largely tonal; and from my guess I shall merely put as
a suggestion to our younger poets, so busy just now with
experiments in technical improvement, that they study
the Chinese variation of tones. It will be hard, but it will
do them no harm; and it may not only lead ahead but
backward to recapture the ancestral union of poetry with
song or melodious recitation—

Sphere-born harmonious sister, Voice and Verse,

which the Puritans almost dissevered when they banished
Chamber Music.

That, however, is speculation at most. I feel on
stronger ground in asserting that a study of the content
of Chinese poetry—which is above all things reflective,
seeking wisdom for its own sake—would surely be medi-
cinal for any European poet in this era of confused alarms,

Where ignorant armies clash by night.

For if Poetry have, in the scope of its divine purpose, an
immediate task just now, it surely is to persuade men that
this warfare they fear, but allow to fascinate them, *is*
ignorance, which to face and despise is *virtue*—the proper
eminence of man above the beasts who scatter in panic
and perish. Now the Chinese hate war simply, finding
it silly. Their few war-poems deal almost exclusively with
the waste of it, the blind marching no-whither, the skele-
tons left and frozen into the sedges. The poet Li Hua of
the eighth century has handed down a famous description
of that waste, with musings on its imbecility, in his *Elegy
on an Ancient Battlefield*:

The Warden shows me and says
'This is an ancient battlefield,
Where army and army have fallen:
At times the wailing of ghosts is heard
When it is cloudy and dark....'

Thus I have heard—
During the state-levies of Ch'i and Wei,
And the conscriptions of Ching and Han,
The soldiers had to march thousands of miles
And remained roofless year after year.
They tended their horses in the morning near sand and water,
They crossed the river at night when it was ice-bound:

The earth and the sky were so far and wide
That they knew not where lay their homeward path.
Their lives were naked to swords and blades,—
To whom could they tell their feelings and thoughts?...

A victor of Chou returns: at the reception feast honours
are conferred amid much drinking 'with proper ceremony
and high manners'. The First Emperor of Ch'in starts to
build the Great Wall and mortars its ten thousand miles
with the blood of his people. The poet comments—

> Regard the numerous people under heaven—
> Is there anyone who has not parents
> Bringing him up and protecting him
> For fear that he might not live long?
> Who has not brothers,
> Helping one another even as hands and feet?
> Who has not husband or wife,
> Kind to each other as guests or friends?
>
> Whether he (the conscript soldier) is alive or dead
> His folk are not sure:
> Even though others bring report
> They still hesitate to believe.
> He is ever in their restless heart and eyes
> Whether they lie awake or in dreams....
>
> What, then, is the escape?
> Peace and good-will with all the neighbouring states.

Equally poignant and persistent recurs the burthen of
lament of soldier and commander, from forts on the far
northern frontier, as yet another winter closes in and the
wild geese are clanging southward and homeward—

> ...the lonely citadel is closed.

A cup of poor wine,—my native land is ten thousand miles
    away;
The Huns have not yet been conquered, I have no power to
    go home.

> The Tartar flute comes wailing over a land frost-bound;
> Hardly can one sleep—
> The general's white hair and the soldiers' tears.

'It would not be an exaggeration to say', writes Mr Arthur Waley, 'that half the poems in the Chinese language are poems of parting or separation, and a great deal of it, to be sure, deals with the sundering of male friends.' But—and with all deference due to a scholar from one who has already confessed his own lack of learning—I must demur, and positively, when he goes on to say that 'to the Chinese the relation between man and woman is something commonplace, obvious—a need of the body, not a satisfaction of the emotions'. In this I am assured (and indeed the body of Mr Waley's own translations supports the assurance) that he is mistaken. Yet how easily—and how much more easily—the similar but converse mistake might be made we may guess if we suppose a Chinese reader deriving his theory of *Western* love between man and woman from the evidence of our poetry. I dare say that nine-tenths of our amatory lyrics deal with the pursuing lover, his ardours or his despairs; whereas in my own observation of normal folk wedlock deepens love at least as often as not—and so deeply that they can no longer chatter about it:

> Passions are liken'd best to floods and streams,
> The shallow murmur, but the deep are dumb.

On this point I, in my turn, may be mistaken. But the love-poetry of China dwells mainly on the growth of attachment after marriage. Until quite recently marriages in that country were arranged by parents or the chiefs of families (a custom not unknown in Western nations). Therefore to understand the Chinese emotion of love one must first consider the immense preponderance of poems that express the agonies of parting, the nostalgia of exile—of exile over distances hardly to be realised by us—and for stretches of time not determinable by the sufferer. It is out of these that his messages come, to reach his home through hazard and delay, if ever. It is then that he speaks his affection; and at pains, not only because the difficult rules of his art command this, but just as any one of us will take more pains when writing to a friend in New Zealand than over a note addressed to someone in the next street. Consciously or not, we say to ourselves, 'This letter is important, having to travel far, and moreover it must convey to X, not in set words but by some under-current of tone, that our friendship, covering time and the bulge of the earth, abides as ever.'

To this must be added the ancient, rooted conviction of his race that the best reward of life is that a man be granted to retire betimes to his own fields and orchards; tilling them, subsisting on their fruits, watching the growth of his children and, in the leisure of a contented household, reading the poets and philosophers to confirm his own assurance of the true ends of existence:

With a bottle and cup I drink alone,
Looking at the trees in the court I ease my heart;
Leaning against the southern window to soothe my high
 thoughts,
I realise that comfort can be found even in the narrowest
 room.

⟨ xv ⟩

I pay a daily visit to my garden as a promenade;
Though I have a door, it is always closed.
With stick in hand I roam about or take rest at will;
At times I lift up my head and gaze at the distance:
The clouds come up freely from the peaks;
The birds, when tired of flying, know their way back.
The sun slowly westers,
While I loiter around a lonely pine.

At last I have come home!
I will have no more of the social intercourses.
The world and I have dropped far asunder;
What after all have I to seek?
Intimate talks with my kinsmen will give me joy,
My delight in my lute and books will keep me from worry

When the farmers tell me of the return of spring,
I set myself to work in the western fields.
To go there, I take a cany wagon
Or row a light boat,
Meandering here and there along dales,
Rambling up and down the hills.
Cheerfully the trees flash to splendour,
Gaily the rivulets brisk along.
Admiring that every phase of nature has its time,
I find my life drawing to its close.

Multiply this individual man by millions, and you get
a people—not morose as Newman once suggested, or
morose only as distrustful of any 'barbarian' intruding
upon its own patient culture refined through ages. In
their turn the Chinese seek neither adventure over-seas
nor (and still less) aggression. A favourite poem, older
than that of Li Hua quoted above—*The Peach-Blossom
Fountain* of T'ao Ch'ien (A.D. 372–427)—tells of a solitary
angler who, following upstream to his river's source,
found it issuing through a cleft in the rock of a mountain,

passed through it, and found himself in a land of hospitable and completely happy villagers. They were a tribe, they informed him, whose ancestors had escaped hither with their wives and families from the Ch'in persecutions of books and learning. They showed no knowledge of the Han, not to speak of the Wei and the Chin dynasties. On hearing of these they were moved to sighs, and when the angler took his leave, enjoined on him 'This is not worth telling to outside folk'. Nevertheless he, deeming that maybe he had mistaken some tributary for the main river, set marks along his way back and arriving home imparted his adventure to the Governor of the City, who sent out a search party, but, whatever had become of the marks, the way could not be found, nor has been. The poet concludes:

> Hidden for five hundred years
> Suddenly one day the Enchanted Land was disclosed;
> But because it was alien to the outer world
> Soon it was shut out again as before.
>
> Tell me, O you seekers after strange lands,
> What do you know beyond this world?

The following pages, while selected to represent the poets of one period, represent also the constant attitude of the Chinese mind, always through centuries pacific. I hope, too, that the reader will find the cadences of Mr Ch'u's rendering as attractive to his ear as they are to mine.

ARTHUR QUILLER-COUCH

Jesus College, Cambridge
March 1937

THE SOUTH COUNTRY

*(Part of South-east China along the southern side
of the Yangtze River)*

I

So all the world praises the South Country to me:
'It best befits you a wanderer there to spend your life.
The waters in spring look bluer than the skies,
And rains will lull you to sleep in the painted boat.

The wine-shop maids are as charming as the moon,
Their glowing arms like frozen frost and drifted snow.
Do not go home before you are old,
Lest you should break your heart.'

II

Now I recall the joys of the South Country:
When I was young and my spring attire was light,
On horseback I roamed by the arched bridge,
And on the terraces red sleeves beckoned at me;

Behind the emerald screen and the gold-knockered doors,
I got drunk and slept amid the thick-growing flowers
    of love.
Were I to see those flowers once again,
Even though my hair grew white, I swear, I would never
    come home.

WEI CHUANG

FOR REMEMBRANCE

FROM the sun-touched hills the mists begin to withdraw,
In the clearing sky the scattered stars look fewer;
The sinking moon still shines on the faces of the lovers,
Who are shedding tears at parting in the early morning.

Much has been said,
Yet we have not come to the end of our feelings;
Looking back she says again:
'If you remember my silken skirt of green,
Have tender regard for the sweet grass wherever you go.'

NIU HSI-CHI

H ER   B I R T H D A Y

A FEAST being spread in spring-time,
With a cup of green wine and a joyous song,
I repeat my salutation and offer my three wishes:
First, may you have a long life;
Second, may I have good health;
Third, may we live as the swallows on the beam,
Happily together all the year round.

FÊNG YEN-CHI

THE FISHERMAN'S SONG

THE spray of waves, as on purpose, makes a thousand
    drifts of snow,
The flowering peach-trees in silence form a regiment of
    spring.
A bottle of wine,
A fishing rod—
How many men upon earth are as happy as I?

A light oar in the spring breeze, a leaf-like boat;
A silken line, a slender hook.
The eyot is spread with flowers,
The goblet filled with wine.
In the wide world of waters liberty is mine.

PRINCE LI YÜ

C O U R T   L I F E

Just after the evening toilet the snow-white flesh shines;
In the Spring Hall the royal maids stand arrayed.
The music of reeds and pipes rings out to the horizon,
While the Song of the Rainbow Skirts is played over again.

On the wind, who is scattering perfumed powder?
I beat tune on the balustrade, drunk and overcome with joy.
On my return make not the candles shine with their red
    flames;
For I go to roam on horseback in the bright moonlight.

Prince Li Yü

THE TRYST

THE flowers bright, the moon dim, and a light mist
    eddying about—
Tonight is meant for me to go to my love.
Off with my stockings, I walk down the fragrant steps,
With my gold-lined slippers in hand.

At the south side of the Painted Hall we meet;
I fall trembling in his arms and say:
'Because it was so hard to come to you,
Let me have your very best caress.'

PRINCE LI YÜ

PAST AND PRESENT

I

THE flowering trees have lost their spring hues,
All too soon!
It can't be helped that it rains fast in the morning and blows
      hard in the evening.

Tears on Her rosy cheeks
Entreat me to stay and get drunk—
Can ever this happen again?
It is destined that life be always full of regret and waters
      for ever flow towards the sea.

II

In silence I go alone up to the Western Chamber,
Above which hangs the sickle-shaped moon;
In the deep, lonely court of paulownia trees is gaoled the
      chilly autumn.

Cut it, yet unsevered,
Order it, the more tangled—
Such is parting-sorrow,
Which dwells in my heart, too subtle a feeling to tell.

PRINCE LI YÜ

SEPARATION

Since my departure, spring is half gone,
Every sight is heart-rending to me.
Below the steps the plum-blossoms fall white like snow;
When brushed away, they cover me over again.

The wild-geese come with no message at all;
Remote is my home, which even dreams can scarcely reach.
The sorrow of separation is like the grass of spring;
The further you travel, the more it grows.

Prince Li Yü

A LOVE-SONG

Her hair is a mass of cloud,
Her teeth are strings of pearls;
In a flowing gown and a light skirt of gauze,
Softly she knits her dark-blue brows.

The autumn wind blows harsh,
To its accompaniment falls the rain,
Beyond the windows are several plantain-trees,—
Oh, how can she bear this weary night!

PRINCE LI YÜ

R E G R E T S

I

BEYOND the curtain the rain drizzles;
Spring is declining.
My silken coverlet is too thin to stand the chill of the
    morning watch.
In a dream I forgot that I was in a strange land,
And indulged myself in merry-making.

Alone in the twilight I lean over the balcony;
Far off lies my native land,
Which it is easy to part from, but hard to see again.
Flowing waters and faded flowers are gone for ever,
As far apart as heaven is from earth.

II

The thought of the past brings me only griefs,
Which will not be banished before my present vision:
The autumn wind sweeps through the court-yard and moss
    grows up the steps.
The pearl screen hangs free and unrolled,—
All day long no one has called on me.

My golden sword has been buried deep,
My valour sunken among chaff and weeds.
In the evening cool and serene the moon spreads her
    radiance,
Reminding me that the shadows of the crystal domes and
    marble halls
Fall blankly upon the River Ch'in-huai.

PRINCE LI Yü

LONGING FOR THE
SOUTH COUNTRY

How sad I was
In my dreams last night!
Just as in the old days, I visited the Royal Park,
Where the chariots ran like swift streams and the horses
  like prancing dragons,
When flowers were blooming and the moon was shining
  in the prime of spring.

PRINCE LI YÜ

THE LAND
OF DRUNKENNESS

Last night there was a storm of wind and rain,
When the blinds and curtains rattled in the autumn air.
The candles burning out, the night watches expiring, now
    I rested on my pillow,
And now sat up, ill at ease.

Worldly affairs go by like running waters;
Our life floats as a dream.
The way to Drunken Land is the only safe one to travel
    often;
Nowhere else is good to visit.

PRINCE LI YÜ

THE EVERLASTING
SORROW*

SPRING flowers and autumn moon, when will you come to
    an end?
And how much do you know of the past?
On my small chamber last night blew the vernal breeze
    once again;
I cannot endure to think of my native land in the moonlight.

The carved balustrades and the marble steps must still be
    there,
But my youthful features have changed.
You ask me, 'How much sorrow do you bear?'
'As much as a whole river in spring flood flowing towards
    the sea!'

PRINCE LI YÜ

* See Note 1 on page 55.

ON THE FRONTIER

ALL aspects change on the Frontier when autumn comes:
Wild-geese fly southward without faltering;
Shouts echo on all sides along the Border when the bugle
    blows;
Amid a thousand mountains,
In the spreading mists and the westering sun, the lonely
    citadel is closed.

A cup of poor wine,—my native land is ten thousand miles
    away;
The Huns have not yet been conquered, I have no power
    to go home.
The Tartar flute comes wailing over a land frost-bound;
One can hardly sleep—
The general's white hair and the soldiers' tears.

FAN CHUNG-YEN

TO A FRIEND

IN my youth I was carefree;
Time flies as an arrow;
So, I have not perceived that the prime of life has gone,
Until now
When I begin to commiserate the moon at the full,
Flowers at the full,
Cups at the full.

While the small boat waits to depart from the willowy
    bank,
We are still rejoicing over the feast.
The sun westers low, the farewell-song is over, men are
    separating;
Leaning on the sandalwood oar
I gaze at the water far away,
The sky far away,
The loved one far away.

SUNG CH'I

PARTING IN AUTUMN

THE cold cicadas sing dolorously;
Beyond the Wayside Pavilion in twilight
A sudden shower has just ceased.
Joyless is the farewell party at the capital,
Where we linger on our parting,
The sandalwood boat is waiting to set sail.
Hand in hand we look at each other with tears in our eyes,
Wordless, sobbing—
To think that I am going across a thousand miles of mists
 and waves,
Where the evening clouds are deepening and the skies
 wide to the south.

Fond lovers from of old are pained by parting,
Which is all the more intolerable in the time of chilly
 autumn.
Tonight when I become sober from wine, where shall I be?
On the willowy banks with the morning wind and the
 waning moon.
During my absence all the year round
Sunny weather and lovely sights will be to me in vain;
Even though I had a thousand tender thoughts,
To whom can I tell them?

LIU YUNG

HOME THOUGHTS

AT evening the pelting rain sprinkles the River and the
    skies,
Rinsing the autumn pure and clear.
The frosty wind grows cold and fierce,
The passes and fords become more desolate
With the setting sun upon the watch-towers.
Here red is gone and green in decay;
Luxuriant nature draws near its close.
Only the mighty River
Runs in silence eastwards to the sea.

I cannot bear gazing from high places
On my native country far, far away,
While my breast is cracking with homesickness.
I wonder, alas! why my footsteps
Have made me tarry year by year.
The fair one, I think,
Must have watched at her chamber window
And mistaken many a homeward boat from the horizon,
Not knowing here I lean over the balcony,
Lost in heavy thoughts.

LIU YUNG

A BLOSSOM

A PEONY blossom bepearled with dew-drops
She plucked and, coming across the court-yard,
Asked her love, smiling:
'Whose beauty excels, the flower's or mine?'

He, in order to tease her,
Gave all his praise to the flower;
She in a moment of girlish anger
Crumpled the blossom and threw it over him.

ANONYMOUS

IN THE FIRST
FULL-MOON NIGHT

LAST year, in the First Full-moon Night,
At the Flower Market, lanterns were as bright as day;
When the moon came up on the tops of the willows,
My love and I met after dusk.

This year, in the First Full-moon Night,
The moon and lanterns are the same as before.
But I do not see the one who was with me last year,
And tears wet the sleeves of my spring gown.

OU-YANG HSIU

A FAREWELL

Rain fell on the trees in the South Country,
Unnumbered flowers came in bloom overnight.
Now the green leaves begin to form shade,
Beneath is the traveller's homeward path.

We rejoice where we meet,
Hiding our minds from the fleeting spring.
With a cup of wine I pray you, O Eastern Wind,
Do not hasten away so soon!

WANG AN-SHIH

AFTER DRINKING

TONIGHT I drank at East Slope,—sobered once, drunk
    again.
On my return, it seems to be the third watch;
My boy-servant already snoring loud,
No one answers my knocking.
Leaning upon my stick, I listen to the sound of the River.

Often I regret that my life is not my own;
When can I become oblivious of worldly affairs?
The night deep, wind silent, waves calm—
O that I might go in a small boat,
To spend the rest of my life on rivers and seas!

SU SHIH

IN MEMORY

FOR ten years the living and the dead have been far
    severed;
Though not thinking of you,
Naturally I cannot forget.
Your lonely grave is a thousand miles away,
Nowhere to tell my grief.
Even if we could meet, you would not recognise me;
My face is all covered with dust,
My hair on the temples shows frosty.

Last night in a dream I returned home,
And, at the chamber window,
Saw you at your toilet;
We looked at each other in silence and melted into tears.
I cherish in my memory year by year the place of heart-
    breaking,
In the moonlight night,
The knoll of short pines.

SU SHIH

DRINKING IN THE MID-AUTUMN NIGHT, 1076

and thinking of my younger brother, Su Ch'ê

WHEN did the moon begin to shine?
Lifting my cup I ask of Heaven.
I wonder in the heavenly palaces and castles
What season it is tonight.
I wish to go up there on the wind,
But am afraid the crystal domes and jade halls
Would be too cold on high.
So I dance with my limpid shadow
As if I were no longer on earth.

Around rich bowers,
Into sweet boudoirs,
Shining upon the inmates still awake,
The moon should have no regrets.
Why is she always at the full when men are separated?
Men have their woe and joy, parting and meeting;
The moon has her dimness and brightness, waxing and
    waning.
Never from of old has been lasting perfection.
I only wish that you and I may be ever well and hale,
That both of us may watch the fair moon, even a thousand
    miles apart.

SU SHIH

ON THE RED CLIFF

*(Where Chou Yü of the Wu State defeated the fleet
of the Wei State in A.D. 208)*

THE waves of the mighty River flowing eastward
Have swept away the brilliant figures of a thousand
   generations.
West of the old fortress,
So people say, is Lord Chou's Red Cliff of the time of the
   Three States.
The tumbling rocks thrust into the air;
The roaring surges dash upon the shore,
Rolling into a thousand drifts of snow.
The River and the mountains make a vivid picture—
What a host of heroes once were!

It reminds me of the young Lord then,
When the fair Younger Ch'iao newly married him,
Whose valorous features were shown forth;
With a feather fan and a silken cap,
Amid talking and laughing, he put his enemy's ships to
   ashes and smoke.
While my thoughts wander in the country of old,
Romantic persons might smile at my early grey hair.
Ah! life is but like a dream;
With a cup of wine, let me yet pour a libation to the moon
   on the River.

SU SHIH

A PLAN FOR THE FUTURE

THE night is clear and taintless,
The moonbeams glitter silver white.
Let me pour my wine to the full,
And floating fame and unstable gains
No more trouble my spirit and mind.
For, ah! they are but horses past a peep-hole,
Sparkles out of a flint,
And persons in a dream.

Though I have in me beautiful thoughts,
To whom can I impart them?
I shall happily enjoy my endowments from Nature,
And, when I return home,
Become an idler,
With a lute,
A bottle of wine,
By a rivulet decked with clouds.

Su Shih

WHERE TRAVELLERS GO

WATERS are eyes that glance bright,
Hills are brows that range blue.
If you ask whither travellers are going,
—Where charming brows and eyes abide.

Not long has Spring left us,
And now in turn I see you off.
If you catch up Spring in the South Country,
Stay with him by all means.

SU SHIH

THE RECLUSE

THE waning moon hangs above the sere paulownia trees,
The clepsydra expires and calm becomes the noisy world.
Alone the Recluse is pacing now and then;
How he resembles the image of a lone wild-swan,—

Startled, up it flies and looks back
As though full of sad thoughts that few will know;
It passes all the barren trees but dwells on none,
And hugs itself at the desolate islet of cold sand.

SU SHIH

THE HOME-COMING

For rice I thinned my waist,
For wine I deserted my home—
Mouth and belly have been a burden to each other.
Oh! I will go back home.
Who has stopped you from doing so?
Now I find that all was wrong, and is right.
The morning dew has not dried up;
A traveller shows my way.
Before the gate my children talk and laugh;
But, ah! the chrysanthemums I planted have withered,
And the pine-trees are growing hoar,—
So is my age!
I am content to repose myself under the small window,
    with the wicket closed,
Or to lean upon my stick looking at the lonely clouds and
    homeward birds:
The clouds rise up with no purpose,
The birds when tired return to their nests,
All of their own accord.

At last, I have come home!
I have forgotten both myself and the world.
With my neighbours I hold no prattle;
In my lute and books I find true happiness.
Sometimes I ramble across the rugged hills or along the
    meandering brooks.
When I see the hidden vales loaded with spring floods
    running gay
And the grass and trees with fresh and cheerful looks,

I feel that my life is drawing to a close.
To think how short a while yet my body has left to stay
in the world,
Why should I not awaken to this,
And still bestir myself for no purpose?
Let me follow but my heart—it matters not where I go
or stop.
I have no wish to enquire where the Immortals live,
Nor have I ambition to acquire wealth and fame.
All I care is to compose and sing by rivers and on moun-
tains,
Or to enjoy my cup and bottle alone.
For life is fate, who is to doubt?
With the tide shall I go, but no risk will I run.

Su Shih

PEONY TIME

I FILL your cup to the brim with green wine and beg you,
    my friend,
Stay for yet a while, do not go in haste.
Two parts of the spring-tide are taken by melancholy,
The third is by wind and rain.

Flowers were blooming, flowers are blown—
How much is left with you and me?
Let us murmur no more but sing out loud.
For who knows in peony-time next year
Where we shall meet each other again?

YEH CH'ING-CH'ÊN

THE SEVENTH NIGHT OF
THE SEVENTH MOON*

(*Herd-boy*)   THE soft clouds make decorations,
The shooting stars play harbinger,—
Far across the Silver River you secretly
    come to me.
Though only once a year we meet in the
    time of sharp wind and chill dew,
We are many times happier than the
    lovers on earth.

(*Weaving Girl*) Our feelings are tender as water,
Our meeting is sweeter than a dream;
It is hard for me to look back on the home-
    ward path from the Blackbirds Bridge.
But if our love for each other will long
    endure,
It makes no difference that we do not live
    together day and night.

CH'IN KUAN

* See Note 2 on page 55.

WEIGHED DOWN

THE wind having stopped, the dust smelling sweet, all
    flowers being faded;
It is growing late, yet I have no intention of making my
    toilet.
Though things remain the same, people do not; all affairs
    of life are drawing to a close:
Tears begin to fall before I can speak.

Having heard that at the Double Stream the face of
    Spring is fair,
I also have a desire to go there rowing;
But am afraid the canoe at the Double Stream
Cannot bear the weight
Of so much grief as mine.

LI CH'ING-CHAO

PLUM-BLOSSOMS

In past days, for the sake of plum-blossoms I was often
    drunk and wandered abroad;
For, holding my sleeves, beauties asked me for new songs:
In light red ink I wrote on their embroidered girdles,
With thick green wine they filled up my emerald goblet.

I am old, things are not as they were.
Among flowers I shun drinking, tears falling on my
    clothes.
Now I only want to shut myself indoors, sleeping,
Regardless of the plum-blossoms flying about like snow.

CHU TUN-JU

SORROW AND FLOWERS

I USED to be held at the halt by beauteous flowers;
Butterflies soaring, orioles singing,
Amid the society of youths, in the Land of Drunkenness,
Carefree, I let Spring pass away.

Now in the South Country Spring is fading.
Where has youth gone?
Compare not sorrow to falling flowers;
Flowers are numbered, sorrow is endless.

CHU TUN-JU

LEANING ON THE
BALUSTRADES

A BLUE-TILED, red-painted small building
On the fragrant greens along the south bank of the River—
After a shower of rain, gusts of cold come through the
    gauze windows,
The pear-blossoms fall scattered at twilight.

I gaze over the water to where it mingles with clouds,
And watch the crows until they become specks.
South, north, east, west, everywhere is grief,
Alone I lean first on one side of the balustrades, then on
    another.

CHU TUN-JU

THE GOLDEN DAYS

BORN and bred at the West Capital in the golden days,
I sang all day long and took no heed of the passing years:
Wandering amid flowers, sleeping in wine-houses;
Visited the Two Peaks on the wind,
Crossed the Three Streams by flying with the snow.

Do not laugh at my withered features and grey temples;
My mind is as keen and vigorous as ever,
Like bright moon in a lake and clear sky in a river.
Is there anyone so free as I,
Who refuse even to be an Immortal?

CHU TUN-JU

L E I S U R E

A SMALL garden
Of a few acres,
Where I plant flowers and bamboos to make ornaments at
    will.
The mallowy hedges and thatched cottages
Suit even a villager's taste.
Whenever I like, I drink by the lake,
Get drunk in the woods.

Simply because I have no cares in my breast,
I enjoy all the pleasant things that come my way.
Content and happy,
I live to the best my few years on earth.
Who says that Fairyland is
Outside this world?

CHU TUN-JU

OLD AGE

I AM happy with my old age:
For I have seen life thoroughly,
Become familiar with all truths,
Penetrated the hidden things of the world;
Obliterated altogether the seas of regret and mountains
    of distress;
Free from the charm of flowers,
And the spell of wine,
Always sober.
When I have eaten, I go to bed;
When I awake, I play my part when my turn comes.

Do not talk of the days gone by and time to come;
In my breast
There are no such things.
I have no mind to become an Immortal, to worship Buddha,
Nor to imitate the restless Confucius.
I am unwilling to argue with you,
Laugh as they will—
So, be it so.
My part performed,
I leave my costume to the silly players.

CHU TUN-JU

A RIVER-LONG LOVE

I LIVE at the upper end of the River,
And at the lower end live you;
Every day I long to see you but cannot,
Though from the same River we drink.

When will the River go dry?
When can my sorrow come to an end?
Only may your heart be like mine,
My love for you will not be in vain.

LI CHIH-YI

SOLITUDE

WHO are sitting in company under the bright window?
Two of us—my shadow and I.
But when the lamp burns out and it is time for sleeping,
My shadow will forsake me too.
Ah, misery!
How forlorn I am!

HSIANG KAO

O N   T H E   R I V E R

Along the River lies a stretch of smooth sand,
On which several thousand houses are gathered.
Where the houses come to an end,
The sky and water meet again at the horizon.

I strain my sight from the towering terrace,
At the hovering gulls going away
And the speck-like crows returning home.
But where is the fisher song that I hear?
Likely enough it is but amid the reed-flowers.

Lü-ch'iu Tz'ǔ-kao

IN MY CAROUSAL

In my carousal I am busy with mirth and laughter—
What time have I to give to my worries?
I found of late that those books of old
Are not to be trusted at all.

Last night I lay drunk beside a pine-tree;
I asked it how intoxicated I was.
Suspecting it came forward to support me,
I pushed it and said, 'Begone!'

HSIN CH'I-CHI

N O W   I   K N O W

IN my youth I had no idea of what sorrow was,
And loved to go up lofty buildings.
Upon the lofty buildings,
For composing new poems I was forced to talk of sorrow

Now I know sorrow thoroughly well,
And am loath to talk of it.
Loath to talk of it,
I say instead: 'What a chilly autumn day!'

HSIN CH'I-CHI

TO THE MOON AT THE
MID-AUTUMN NIGHT

THE disc of autumnal glory goes round in silvery ripples,
The 'flying mirror' polished once again.
Lifting up my cup I call to Goddess Ch'ang-o:
'Look how I am mocked by my hoary hair. Tell me what
     to do.'

O would I were riding on the wind,
Traversing the celestial spheres for a thousand miles
And looking down upon the mountains and rivers;
Or were able to strike down the tree that grows in the
     moon,
And let more light, as men fancy, to the earth.

HSIN CH'I-CHI

WALKING BY THE STREAM

WALKING by the stream, fair images I see:
At the bottom of the stream low lies the sky;
Across the sky are sailing clouds,
And within the clouds I find myself.

Who is following my merry song?
The sound arises from the hollow vale.
It is no music from spirits or fairies,
But the bubbling water bearing peach-blossoms on.

HSIN CH'I-CHI

M Y S O R R O W

M Y sorrow has of late become as great as heaven;
Who will pity me?
No one will pity me;
After all I have to take sorrow as my heaven.

All the world's affairs both old and new
I leave to the care of sorrow;
Leaving everything to sorrow,
I move and make my abode at the Fountain of Wine.

HSIN CH'I-CHI

LIFE IN THE CUP

I WILL spend my life in my cup,
All else is empty to me.
From of old only a handful of heroes are known;
Wind-swept and rain-beaten, where are those
Palaces of Han and Castles of Ch'in?

In a dream I joined a band of youthful playmates,
Singing and dancing in a whirl.
At midnight the old monk mistakenly gave a ring of bells,
I was waked up beyond the western window and could
     sleep no more,
When a gust of autumn wind was heard sweeping by.

HSIN CH'I-CHI

TO MY CHILDREN

THE world passes before my eyes like clouds and mists,
It is time for my tottering aged body to decay.
Now what will befit me best?
—To drink, to roam and to sleep.

Pay your taxes early, when they are due;
Live and spend within your means.
Now I still have some things in my charge—
Of bamboos, of hills and of streams.

HSIN CH'I-CHI

A B S E N C E

TIMELY in the morning,
Timely in the evening,
Even twice I see the sea-tides everyday,
But you are always absent from me.

Punctually coming,
Punctually going,
Even the swallows return in mid-May,
But your home-coming is never known.

LIU K'Ê-CHUANG

FLOWERY QUESTIONS

FLUTTERING like the light pinions of the butterflies,
Scattering like blood-red drops—
If the Lord of Heaven has no love for flowers,
What do these charms and beauties mean?

In the morning we see them richly deck the branches;
In the evening we see the branches growing thin.
If the Lord of Heaven really loves flowers,
Why are they borne away by wind and rain?

LIU K'Ê-CHUANG

S P R I N G

THE vernal skies are spread with dismal clouds;
Beneath the apple-trees the eastern wind blows foul.
Spring has not so tender a heart as I,
Who watch the blossoms, wishing them never to decay.

Deliberately I spend the spring days in my emerald cup;
But, alas! when I am sobered, my griefs come fresh as ever.
I humbly beseech you, Eastern Wind:
Do not blow hard upon the flowers,
Why not blow my griefs away?

KUAN CHIEN

YOU AND I

You and I
Love each other so
As from the same lump of clay
Is moulded an image of you
And one of me.
In a moment of ecstasy
We dash the images to pieces,
Put them in water,
And with stirring and kneading
Mould again an image of you
And another of me.
There and then,
You will find yourself in me,
I myself in you.

KUAN TAO-SHÊNG

DRINKING BENEATH THE BLOSSOMING TREES

BEFORE the flowers came forth I often made enquiries
    about them;
When they began to bloom I was in fear of wind and rain.
Since wind and rain have done no harm to the flowers
    blowing,
Why should we not come and get drunk beneath the
    blossoming trees?

While this year is with us, let us make no plans for the
    next;
For tomorrow has nothing to do with today.
Look! the vernal breeze, as if admonishing us at the feast,
Lets a petal of blossom drop before our eyes.

LIU YIN

THE MASTER OF THE
WESTERN LAKES

Roving amid mists and waves,
I style myself the Master of the Western Lakes.
With a gentle breeze pushing my small oar,
I row out of the Cove of Reed-flowers.

In high spirits, loudly I sing,
Swelling the tranquil night with full-lunged sound.
No one praises me;
I clap my hands alone,
And a thousand mountains echo my song and applause.

Bhikshu Chêng Yen

NOTE 1 (see page 13)

Prince Li Yü (also known as Li Hou Chu) was the last ruler of the Southern T'ang Dynasty (A.D. 937–975), whose capital was Nanking. When afterwards the city was captured by the First Emperor of the Sung Dynasty (960–1296) he was taken prisoner and detained in Pienliang (now Kaifeng), where he died two years later. He wrote probably all but the first three poems in his exile, and story says that it was for the line 'I cannot endure to think of my native land in the moonlight' in the last poem that he was put to death with poisoned wine. His masterly style tinged with subtle lyricism and profound sadness has won him the foremost place in the field of the tz'ŭ-form of poetry.

NOTE 2 (see page 31)

East of the Silver River (Milky Way), so the legend says, lived the Weaving Girl, the grand-daughter of the Emperor of Heaven. She toiled year in and year out in weaving the 'cloud-embroidered heavenly dress'. The Emperor of Heaven seeing that she was diligent and lonely had pity on her and married her to the Herd-boy who lived west of the Silver River. After she was married she gave up her weaving. The Emperor became angry and made her, as a penalty, go back to the east of the River, on condition that she was allowed to go and see the Herd-boy at the west of the River only once a year on the seventh night of the seventh moon. Every year, when the night came, the blackbirds would of themselves gather together into a bridge over the Silver River, across which the Weaving Girl was thus enabled to meet the Herd-boy. And on the same night, on earth, girls would hold parties, offering sacrifice to the Weaving Girl (and the Herd-boy?) and wishing that she would bestow upon them skill in weaving and needlework and (above all) a good future husband—hence the 'Festival of Wishing for Skill'.

Printed in the United States
By Bookmasters